C000120814

Tongue Fu

Interpersonal Teachings From An
Improv Master For Work and Life

Justin Howard

© 2021 Justin Howard

All rights reserved. No portion of this book may be reproduced in any form without permission from the publisher.

Acknowledgements

My family offers me unending support and tolerance for my unhinged endeavors. My wife Brittany, my daughter Audrey, and my son Lucas who ride willingly with me into all levels of adventure. My parents Gary and Debbie who painstakingly helped mold me into who I am. And my sister Jennifer, the smartest and most resilient of us all.

My other family, all those who've graced the doors of The Black Box Improv theater. There is little scarier than an improv stage. Those who followed me into that fear, I am forever grateful.

Finally, anyone who counts themselves my friend, has undoubtedly consciously decided to take me for all my shortcomings. I love you for that.

For those who have ditched me along the way, I extend to you the most forceful middle finger that one can muster.

Contents

Introduction

Here we go. Who am I? Who's asking these questions? Isn't it the Author? Yes, it is. Who's the Author?

I'm Glad You Asked

First, I'm writing this halfway into a pandemic. That makes me feel like I'm going to get some slack from the reader. Thank you in advance. Being that this is the case, I hope you'll not see the following as bragging, but a reflection on what was. I also hope that you'll see it as a reasonable set of credentials, enough that you'll give this book a shot.

My name is Justin Howard, and I don't know what my title should be. As I write this, I'm waiting to see what will happen. I'm sure that will affect who I am. As for what I was, that's hard to nail down too.

In July 2012, I opened an improv comedy theater in Dayton, Ohio. Yep, Dayton. I grew up just north of Dayton. I also thought I could will anything to happen. Turns out I wasn't wrong, at least in this case. It opened on Friday July 13th of 2012 and I closed the doors on Friday March 13th of 2020. From now on, I'll just expect my world to flip every Friday the 13th. But hey, we made it almost 8 years and the week before we closed; we had performances on 4 nights, up to 6 classes operating each week across two theater spaces. 80+ performers and a community 200+ strong. And it was cool. The people were cool. Not all of them, but overall pretty cool.

We did some cool stuff there. We didn't collect the best improv comedy community, they all went to a big city to make it. We created the best improv comedy community. And we were good. I'm proud of that part of my life.

In addition to sustaining an improv theater in an unlikely location, I also launched a corporate training company. Crossing my fingers on this one continuing, but who knows. It started accidentally, really. A good friend left the Air Force for Harvard Business School. He got there and basically forced me to come do training for his peers. That was fun. They gave me a standing ovation, and it made me feel significant. That was nice. I hope you have moments like that in life. Word of that experience got out and one thing led to another. I've now worked with the military, some of the largest hospitals in the U.S., and many Fortune 500 companies. I had even become a preferred vendor for one of the biggest and most storied companies in the world's history.

I suppose I should address the title of this book, *Tongue Fu*. It's funny first of all, and to me, that should be enough of a reason. It didn't make the pile of other funny titles that I discarded, because it connected to some core ideas that I express in this book and in my work in general. Kung Fu is a storried Chinese Martial Art as many of you know. In China, Kung Fu can also be a way to talk about any type of practice that takes time and focus and perseverance to master. As such, improv, and the communication tenants at its core, are Kung Fu. As for the Chinese characters (Hanzi) below my name, that was the name given to me by my Chinese professor in college. And yes, that is me on the cover. I have the utmost respect for Chinese culture, so I hope my depiction of a Kung Fu master does not offend anyone. Also, you should know that this book isn't oriented toward that culture at all, I do address this early on in this book.

Though I cannot convey everything I teach in writing in a way that replicates being in a class I teach, this book is a small glimpse into the world of communication as I understand it. I believe the things in this book, if implemented, could make a major difference in your life. I hope you enjoy it. It's been a pain in the ass to write.

3

Let's Get Things Straight

Interactions Of Consequence

Early in this book I'm going to address the nature of questions, but before I do, it's probably best that I remove some of your questions before we even get started. What I'm going to teach in this book about statements is not necessarily meant to apply to all conversations, though I think you will find it could apply to most. This book is

An interaction of consequence is any interpersonal interaction one has with another person that could result in a positive or negative outcome.

meant to address an aspect of communication that specifically relates to interactions of consequence. An interaction of consequence is any interpersonal interaction one has with another person that could result in a positive or negative outcome. It doesn't matter if it's positive or negative. I think sometimes we associate the word consequence with a negative outcome, it just needs to be consequential. If you stop by the desk of one of your coworkers to check in and see how their weekend was, I wouldn't consider that consequential. However, if that coworker is somebody that you need to convince to be on board with an idea you have, that interaction becomes consequential. Typically, it's easy to know that a conversation has consequences because there is a bit more anxiety than normal. Consequential interactions inherently have higher stakes.

That said, in some examples I give throughout this book I will frame up in inconsequential interactions just so you can see how powerful and useful statements can really be.

I would also like to note that I'm writing this book for an individualistic western culture. Many cultures around the world are more collectivist than indivudualist. I'm no expert on world cultures, so I won't be addressing them. If you work with or interact with individuals from different cultures, please understand that some of the concepts in this book shouldn't be applied in those interactions.

Communication Is Not A Volume Game

I'm assuming at this point you have already identified that this is a smaller than typical business self-help book. That's intentional. Nearly every business book I have read seems to be 10% information and 90% fluff. My assumption that the fluff exists to appease a publisher or to achieve a price point. Or maybe the author just enjoys rambling on about things. I think it detracts from the message that a lot of authors are trying to convey. Communication is not about volume. Though you would think it is, considering how in your educational experience you were likely pushed to speak for longer periods of time and to write longer papers. Though I don't think most people spend time consciously thinking about it, I think most people associate excellent communicators with lots of words. Communication is a precise art form. It's about delivering exactly what your audience needs to hear, exactly how they can best receive it, exactly when it needs to be delivered. There are many aspects of this, some of them behavioral, but I think this book will make accessible one of the more foundational aspects of communication that I have rarely seen people take advantage of.

Understanding and Knowing

My wife recently went back to college and was fearful of math requirements because she remembers vividly how much she struggled with math in her youth. One night when we were discussing this, she informed me that not only was she bad at math, but she was a bad test taker. I have heard people say they are bad test takers, and though I understand that there are people in the world who deal with anxiety on such a high level that it would cloud their ability to take a test, I think for most people are mischaracterizing the state that they find themselves in when taking a test. It is my belief that most people who consider themselves bad test takers, experience a combination of increased anxiety because of being tested, and a realization that they didn't really know the content. I think people frequently blur the difference between understanding and knowing. If you were in a math class and your professor explains a concept to you and as she explains it you understand it in that moment, you don't know it yet. You simply understand it, and if you take a test a few days later you will experience the anxiety of

...people frequently blur the difference between understanding and knowing.

trying to recall something that you understand but don't know. Knowing comes from practice, from repetition. Knowing is the ability to do something without needing to recall how to do it. In some ways, knowing is to be cerebral. A professional basketball player knows how to play the game, they don't have to stop and think about how to dribble or how to shoot a basketball. A young child at a basketball camp gains understanding. It's what happens between understanding and knowing that makes all the difference. The professional basketball player took their understanding and worked diligently to repeat it until they knew it. Until it got to where with the game on the line, it didn't fail them. Most of us know addition and subtraction. We were given understanding at a relatively young age, but from that point on we were constantly asked to practice it. It occurs in all varieties of math instruction, so the rest of our educational experience was spent doing addition and subtraction. It also exists in life constantly. When we are buying or selling things, when we are organizing, when we try to decide if we have time to run an errand between appointments. And so, if I gave you a test on simple addition and subtraction, and made your loved ones' lives dependent upon you passing, I am betting most of you would. Because you know it. You can read this book
and every other business book on the market, but if at some point you don't decide to practice what you learned, you will never know it and it will never benefit you.

That sounded a bit like a reprimand, so now here's some really positive news. Out of all the things you do in your life, communication is one that you do almost constantly from the time you wake until you go to bed. It's not like learning how to play the guitar where you have to find 30 minutes of alone time to practice. You can practice this all throughout your day and I think by the time the book is over, you will have a very clear understanding of what it is you need to do and how you can implement it. Communication is a competency that most every company I have interacted with struggles to find in their workforce. If you invest your energy into being a better communicator, you will start down the path differentiation between yourself and your peers.

Quick Summary

Interactions Of Consequence

- An interaction of consequence is any interpersonal interaction one has with another person that could result in a positive or negative outcome.

Communication Is Not A Volume Game

- Communication is a precise art form. It's about delivering exactly what your audience needs to hear, exactly how they can best receive it, exactly when it needs to be delivered.

Understanding and Knowing

- ...people frequently blur the difference between understanding and knowing.

- Out of all the things you do in your life, communication is one that you do almost constantly from the time you wake until you go to bed.

Question Everything

Nature Of Questions

In my time doing corporate training, I hear about questions all the time. I'm not saying that I hear people asking questions, I'm saying that I hear people talking about how important questions are. There have been several times in my training where I am teaching a group about listening skills or helping them understand how to think more quickly on their feet, and someone will interject and say "I even see how there could be a lot of application in this with asking great questions". There are books about the importance of questions, there are books about how to create great questions, there are even books that just give a bunch of questions to memorize.

Admittedly, this caught me off guard a little because in the world of improv, questions are generally bad. In improv, where you have no or little information, a question is simply creating a space where that information could be. If an improviser says to another improviser:

"What did you do last night?"

The improviser is creating a space where information could be about what happened last night. That may sound good, but what it does is force the other improviser to be creative about a fictional circumstance. In improv there was no last night. There is no right now. We're making this up completely, so when we ask a question, all we're really doing is placing the onus of the scene on the other person. Doing this creates a hiccup in the interaction.

When you ask someone a question, you are asking them to retreat into their head

When you ask someone a question, you are asking them to retreat into their head for a moment. They do this in part because questions often come out very simply, but the response is often complex. The first complexity of response is the complexity of the thing you were asking. If you were part of a party

12

planning committee at your workplace and you say:

"What do you guys think about hanging streamers from the ceiling?"

This is not just a simple question to answer. It requires the other person or people to imagine the streamers, to consider the cost and how they will be acquired, think about how they will be attached, and try to project how they will be received by the partygoers. Suddenly something that sounded really simple when asked, actually comes with a fair amount of complexity. The other complexity of their response lies in their internal debate over how much they want to reveal to the person who asked the question. If you were in sales and you ask:

"Do you have a budget for this?"

Although the answer may seem like it's a simple yes or no, there's a good chance that how they respond to that question will be based on how much they want others to know about the money that they have to spend. This is when a response to a question becomes filtered. And there are many filters that can apply to an answer when one is not entirely trusting of the other person and where they're headed. This even

happens with people you actually trust. If your spouse
or your child comes up to you and says:

"Do you love me?"

Hopefully this is a simple answer for you, but an
immediate thought that enters your mind is:

"What do they want?"

The more trusting an individual is in an
interaction, the more willing they are to lose the filter
and answer honestly and authentically. Since business
people like charts, I have made a chart for study below:

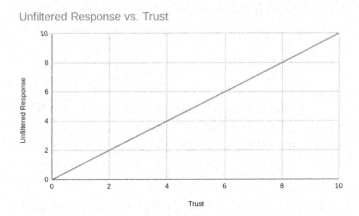

Unfiltered Response vs. Trust

You can see in the chart I made, because I
think this is true, that the more trusting someone is, the
more likely they are to give an unfiltered response. I

know what you're thinking, people trust me. No, they don't. One might be a trustworthy person, but that doesn't mean that people will not question motives.

It's important that you understand how it is biologically that people retreat into their own heads. There are mechanisms that your brain activates to keep you safe in a variety of situations. Imagine that you're gardening one day in the spring and you lift a rock. Under the rock is an angry-looking snake. Before you can even really *The more trusting an individual is in an interaction, the more willing they are to lose the filter and answer honestly and authentically.* consciously process what you're looking at, your brain will have already elevated your heart rate and your breathing and probably will have almost instantaneously withdrawn your hand from that rock. You don't control these processes; they happen before you can really think about your situation. This is a part of the fear response. It activates when the human brain faces uncertainty. Certainty is a major component of trust. See the pie chart below:

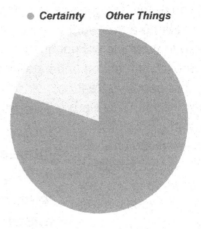

● Certainty   Other Things

Strategic Questions

Though I'm not interested in jumping on the "create great questions" bandwagon, I am not saying that they have no value. They absolutely can have value, but in interactions of consequence I would encourage one to think of questions as strategic. When I'm on my game in interactions, I only ask questions for a few reasons.

I will ask questions if I am sure that the question is simple and inconsequential. I make sure that it is easy to answer and does not give them a reason to be in their head. A question like:

"I saw something on social media, did you go two a soccer game this weekend?"

This is easy for them to answer; it doesn't require that they retreat into their head. That type of question can often help build rapport and put people at ease.

Another reason I'll ask a question is if I don't care about the answer, but the suddenness of the question, I believe, will make them unconsciously respond nonverbally. I use this in sales occasionally when someone is diligent about not providing information. But it's really important that I don't care about their answer because a question that makes them respond nonverbally almost always drives them into their heads.

Do I want the other person to get in their head, filtering their response?

The last reason that I will use a question in an interaction of consequence is because I want them to go deep into their head and over-analyze. Sometimes it's a great way to persuade someone. In fact, counselors and coaches use questions almost exclusively for trying to get you to think critically about how you would answer something. This is when you are trying to get someone to realize something about themselves or an issue that they don't seem to have been able to realize prior. I've heard many sales trainers teach questions like:

"Do you really want to put your family in a minivan with lesser safety standards?"

That kind of question invites the person being sold to disengage from a stalemate on an issue and instead think and analyze the weight that they are putting in their family safety over maybe price. Questions are also good ways to get someone to commit to a lesser sale along the way to the overall sale.

If you finish reading this book and agree with my assessment of questions and statements, my advice to you is that you think about questions in this last way:

Do I want the other person to get in their head, filtering their response?

If the answer is no, then don't ask them a question because that's exactly where you'll send them.

Though maybe this is more applicable to sales professionals, I think it can be true in the early parts of most interactions. I was teaching a sales team, and as a group they do the bulk of their work on the phone making business-to-business cold calls. I asked them

18

to tell me the very first thing that they say to the prospective client, and universally they all offered a question. Most of the questions sounded something like:

"Hey Tina, it's so-and-so from such-and-such company, do you have a couple minutes that we can talk?"

What the sales professionals didn't understand is that they are not asking that question at all. In fact, their prospective client is hearing a different question entirely. You can expect that if they hear a different question, they are going to respond to a different question than the one you asked. The question they hear is:

"Hey Tina, do you want to be in a sales interaction right now?"

And if that's the question that the prospective client is hearing, you can understand why so few of them could make headway with that first call. I mean, think about the times you have driven onto a used car lot to kill time or satisfy curiosity and the salesperson comes approaching you. It really does not matter what they say, it's likely your answer is:

"Oh I'm just looking" or "I'm just killing time."

Though those may be true statements, the sales person likely asked you something like:

"Are you looking for a little more room for the family?" or "Are you in the market for a car that has better gas mileage?"

Your answers weren't an answer to his or her question, they were an answer to:

"Want to deal with a car salesperson?"

When you put yourself in this circumstance, you can see how a very filtered response comes in a moment with very little trust. There is no reason to trust the other person on the phone there's and no reason to trust the car salesperson. Not in the beginning.

Questions Are A Cop-Out

That title sounds more provocative than it really is. I'm not accusing you of copping out by asking a question, but trying to explain that it's a *...your brain wants to be comfortable* mechanism the brain uses to cop out of an uncomfortable situation. We've talked so far about the impact of a question on another person, but we haven't talked about the propensity for you to want to ask questions. Questions are one thing that we talk about in the first few classes of improv training. At the theater, after understanding the impact of a question on an improv scene, every person I have ever taught goes on to ask 3 million questions over the course of the class. Most of them get it out of their mouth and will audibly say on stage in the middle of a scene "oh crap, that was a question". Even when you know you're not supposed to do it, your brain wants to do it. Something you should really understand is that your brain wants to be comfortable. It wants you to be comfortable. It works very hard to keep you comfortable, and in most cases does so without ever asking your permission. If you are too hot, you start sweating. If you're too cold, you start shivering. The same thing is true of communication interactions. As soon as your brain feels uncomfortable, it immediately tries to get comfortable. A stage and no script is a very uncomfortable place to be, but I don't think it's that different from the unscripted nature of business life and the stages we find ourselves on, in front of prospective clients, managers and so on. A question for your brain is like a tennis player lobbying a ball back over. It puts the responsibility on the other person and it gives you what feels like time to compose yourself. And so if you choose to go down the path of changing the way you communicate regarding questions and statements, please know that you are by default a question machine and your brain will do it without you giving it permission in most cases. So the failure rate on changing something like this is exceptionally high. But I think you'll see through the rest of this book the impact that statements can have, and even if you could only replace a question with a statement every once in a while in your interactions, you are slowly chipping away at a behavior that has been burnt into you for your entire lifetime. I also think that even if you can only do a few statements here and there, you'll find them to be to your benefit and the more you do it the better you will get at some point. This is how you go from understanding to knowing.

Quick Summary

Nature Of Questions

- When you ask someone a question, you are asking them to retreat into their head.

- The more trusting an individual is in an interaction, the more willing they are to lose the filter and answer honestly and authentically.

Strategic Questions

- Do I want the other person to get in their head, filtering their response?

Questions Are A Cop-Out

- ...your brain wants to be comfortable.

Make A Statement

Nature Of Statements

Statements can often do the work that one intends with the question, while engaging a person's brain completely differently. Statements activate different parts of the human brain and have proven out over generations to be an excellent mechanism for moving an improvisation seen forward. Since all of your interactions are improvised as well, consider, if you will, the statement.

Statements Supply Information

The first thing that statements offer that questions do not is information. Specifically, they supply information about the thing one wishes to engage the other person about. Information, or the lack thereof, is a major factor in uncertainty, and thus, trust.

If someone wants you to do something fun but won't tell you what it is, the lack of information about what you're going to get yourself into is a major factor in your mistrust of your friend and the fun they tell you you'll be having. If you can recall the spellbinding graph in the prior chapter...you can't? I'll just put it in here again:

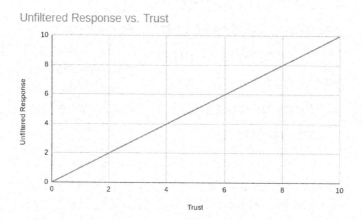

If information provided in a statement increases his trust, then we are increasing our ability to get an honest and unfiltered response from the other person.

In the next chapter, I will go into great detail about the components of really good statements. I'll teach you how to supply information in clever ways when constructing your statements. I know all of this sounds academic right now, but when you see how to construct a really strong statement, I think you'll be able to see how, in time, this could become cerebral for you.

Statements Leave A Vacuum

If questions cause people to retreat into their head to process and analyze, a statement does the exact opposite. In fact, it's almost as if between you and the other person there is a vacuum that sucks words straight out of their face. Ridiculous, I know.

If questions cause people to retreat into their head to process and analyze, a statement does the exact opposite.

But both in improvisation and in interpersonal interactions, when faced with a statement, individuals are far more likely to respond quickly and with little thought. Consider my prior example of a partner or child asking you "do you love me?". Now consider the alternative. Imagine if they just walked into a room and said "I love you". When someone simply states "I love you.", it doesn't create in you nearly the feelings of mistrust and "what are they up to?", or "what do they want?". Often, when someone says that to you you'll just simply reply with "I love you too". It's almost like making a statement is pushing someone down a hill. They just start rolling.

This vacuum doesn't really do anything to build trust, but seems to circumvent it. It's almost as if the other person's brain doesn't flag what was said as something worthy of analysis. If we couple that with the information that the statement gives them, statements are really powerful tools of communication. But there is one

Shut up. It heightens the gravity of the vacuum.

very important thing that creates a vacuum. You have to shut up. After you make a statement if someone doesn't immediately respond you'll feel the urge to explain yourself or add a bit more information or even follow up with the question like "you know?". Don't do it, don't give in. Shut up. It heightens the gravity of the vacuum. More on that later.

My in-person workshops focus on things like listening skills, and when I teach this, I quote a few studies that really prove out that nobody is really listening to anyone. And if that's even partially true, you can imagine that with most people, the desire to have anyone listen to them about anything is probably relatively high. It has been my experience that I can be in a grocery store waiting in line to

When in the vacuum, people wind up saying giving up all sorts of unfiltered information.

check out, and if I say something to the person in front

of me like "I see I'm not the only one who indulges in Swiss rolls.", the other person almost automatically launches into a conversation with me. It's almost as if I gave them the green light to be heard. It's amazing. Usually when I get done with that conversation, I wind up saying something like well I'll pray for you and your family. When in the vacuum, people wind up saying giving up all sorts of unfiltered information. Even very personal information. Don't be surprised if you practice this and find that it opens the floodgates in conversation.

I mean, isn't the point of a great question to get back great information? I like to think of conversations like a series of improv scenes, where each different subject in the conversation is a scene. If you make a statement, what you are essentially doing is pushing other people into the scene you want them to be a part of. When you ask a question, they retreat into their heads and strategically try to steer the conversation in the direction they want it to go.

Examples Of Questions Turned Into Statements

Q: *Do you think it would be a good idea if we break down the distinct elements of the project and each take one or two?*

In this question, you're asking them to evaluate the merit of the idea of splitting up the work. It's an invitation to think about the room and how it would work amongst its members. It also invites them to evaluate whether it would be in their own best interest to do so. Look at an alternative statement:

S: *Breaking this project down into its distinct elements and dividing them up can be a good way to get things done efficiently.*

In this way, you've lured them into a simple agree or disagree proposition. Anyone with a desire to contribute or a strong feeling one way or the other will jump in quickly and with little thought.

Q: *Hey Thad, what's going on with the TPS report that was due yesterday?*

Thad immediately starts looking for ways to filter his response. He might try to gauge the harm that could come his way, he might weigh political fall

out if he names a coworker that is holding things up. We could list many potential filters.

S: *Hey Thad, the TPS report was due yesterday.*

Thad isn't being asked to explain himself. He's being forced to respond to the factual nature of the statement. That's a quick vacuum to get sucked into. Unfortunately for Thad, once he takes the speaking stick to acknowledge the facts, he'll explain the circumstances without the ability to measure his response. This statement doesn't create comfort for Thad. Thad has it coming and I think we can all see that.

Q: *How big of an undertaking do you see this being?*

Sometimes questions can imply opinion, but do so vaguely. Is it a problem for this person if the project is a big undertaking? How do I need to convince them it's not? These are some internal analyses this question creates.

S: *This seems like it could be a pretty big undertaking.*

Again, we're forcing them to agree or disagree with the statement. You're very likely to get a "yes, but...." or a "yes, and..."

 Finally, an improv guy writing a book said the phrase "Yes, and". If you already knew one thing about improv, you've been waiting this whole time for it. Everybody likes to talk about "Yes, and" with improv. Rightfully so, it's an important tool we use to move scenes forward. If you're unaware, "Yes, and" simply means to agree with the other improviser (that's the "Yes") and add more information (that's the "And"). This is something I'll not be getting into in this book. Learning how and where to use that phrase is more complicated than most people understand. It is, however, worthy of referencing regarding how people respond to statements.

In our improv classes, students struggle to implement "Yes, and", especially early on. As they get more comfortable on stage and with their fellow improvisers, it comes out much more naturally. I think this is because we do it in our daily lives all the time. When we are comfortable with the person in the interaction, it flows out. Listen for it in the world around you. Sometimes you have to look for more than just the words. If someone says "look at this amazing window display", the respondent is likely to say something like:

"Oh my god, look at the detail in the miniature houses."

That person didn't literally say "yes" or "and" but their statement could easily be rewritten as:

"**Yes**, that is an amazing display **and** the miniature house has a lot of detail."

This phrasing actually gets used a lot in conversations, and the more comfortable you can make them, the more you'll hear it falling out of the right faces.

Quick Summary

Statements Leave A Vacuum

- If questions cause people to retreat into their head to process and analyze, a statement does the exact opposite.

- Shut up. It heightens the gravity of the vacuum.

- When in the vacuum, people wind up saying giving up all sorts of unfiltered information.

Statement Starter Kit

Start In The Middle

This is an old adage in the world of improv. God only knows who first came up with this phrase, but it has served improv shows for a very long time. The idea is that one should create a statement that starts in the middle of the subject one wishes to discuss as opposed to the beginning. I have found in teaching improv that almost everyone struggles to do this. Let me give an example of how it occurs on an improv stage.

Let's pretend that an improviser has an idea for a scene she wants to initiate. In her mind, she wants to be a nervous murderer getting supplies from a hardware store to take care of a body. Here's what her initiation would look like if she didn't start in the middle of that idea:

"Hi, quaint little hardware store you have here."

With this initiation, our improviser started at the beginning of the idea of being in a hardware store and with that delivered a generic hello to the other improviser. The reason this is something we want to avoid an improv is that the other improviser will respond to that statement and may do so in a way that makes her scene idea impossible. Here's an example of how the other improviser may respond:

"Thank you, we are a pacifist hardware store so we only sell things that could not be used in the harm of another person. We mostly sell edible seeds, but not enough that someone could choke."

Just like that, the scene has headed another direction. When you initiate a conversation with someone, especially if it's purposeful, it's like your scene you're initiating. So, you can think about your statement as an improviser would think about their initiation. Starting in the middle of a subject not only creates a vacuum with your statement, but it forces those you're in a conversation with to reply to the circumstances you laid out as opposed to taking your initiation another direction.

Let's say that you manage a group of people and you task a few of them with working together on a project. Let's assume for this example, the project is in complete disarray and the members of the team are at odds with one another. Let's say that you sit them down together in a room because you want to know what is going on. And because you've gotten this far in the book, you know better than to open with a question, especially something like "can someone tell me what's going on here?". Instead you decide to initiate things with a statement, but you didn't initiate in the middle you initiated in the beginning. Here's the example:

"It's come to my attention that there are some issues we need to discuss with this project."

That statement probably sounds pretty good, but it is the type of statement that would typically happen at the very beginning of an interaction. Take a second to re-read that and think of three possible different responses. Could you come up with three different responses that would take the conversation in three different directions potentially? Of course you did. There are almost an infinite number of things that could be brought up in response to that. Let's try one that starts in the middle:

"There are some issues about this project I want to discuss. First is the timeline. Scott, you volunteered to make sure we were adhering to the timeline."

Hard stop. A statement like that, whether delivered at the onset of the conversation or at any point, specifically moves the conversation into one subject area and reduces the different directions that they could take it. It's also isolated one person and created a vacuum such that they will probably start speaking as opposed to thinking.

Teaching this concept has proven to be pretty difficult. It's not that difficult to get people to understand it, but more so difficult to get them to deliver statements that start in the middle. I think there are a few reasons for this. Predominantly we can attribute a lot to the unconscious working of the human brain. Statements that start in the middle tend to feel a little more uncomfortable. Not because they're necessarily abrasive, but because in doing so you're putting more of yourself out there. It creates a feeling of vulnerability, something that our brains intuitively work very hard against. I also think that it feels more polite to start at the beginning. By providing less information and directing the conversation less, it feels as if you were being a more equitable conversation member. And though I think there is a lot of positive to say for that mentality, you're looking for an answer and I don't know that that's all that more polite. The effectiveness of statements largely boils down to your ability to keep someone from retreating into their head and getting them to respond to you in an unfiltered or less filtered way. There's plenty of time to be polite in other aspects of conversation.

A Baseline

Improvisation on a stage, in front of an audience, is more difficult than the improvisation faced in work and life. There is a baseline of information that needs to be clear in order for others to engage. In improv, we need to create and solidify three elements that don't exist until we talk: who, what, and where. The "where" is almost always provided for you in your interactions. In real life, the "where" is simply the setting where the interaction is taking place. That's always provided. In improv, we do all of our scenes on a generic stage with only chairs as props. So for us, we have to create the "where" every time. The "what" is the thing you're doing. So if you are in a conference room sharing updates about your various departments, that's your "what". In improv we also have to create that, usually from just a one-word suggestion. The

The more established your relationships with the people in the interaction, the more potentially comfortable the conversation can be.

"who" however is the one element of our conversational baseline that everyday life and work share with improvisation.

The "who" is of course who all the people in the interaction are. But it represents much, much more. The "who" is about the relationships between the individuals in the interaction. In relationships, they are varying depths of character apparent to one another. Think of five people who you consider your friends. Now think of each friendship and think about what makes your friendship with that person unique to the other friendships you have with the other people you just thought of. Go down the line and do that with each friend. Hopefully, you have found that as you described each friendship, though I'm sure they're similar, they are also unique. The more established your relationships with the people in the interaction, the more potentially comfortable the conversation can be. The more comfortable, the more trust that exists, and thus a higher likelihood of unfiltered responses.

If relationships in the interaction are not well established, focusing on the "who" is a great way to build statements. The more information you provide about yourself, the more likely that others reciprocate, but also the more trustworthy you become to them. This isn't something that we consciously think, rather calculations that our unconscious mind is making about the potential danger of a situation. The more that someone is comfortable with me in an interaction, the more likely they are to drop their defenses.

I, You, We

We teach a really great mechanism in my theater to help improvisers orient their mind toward building information regarding relationships. We will put two improvisers on stage and tell them they can only start statements with the words I, you, or we. Then we toss them a one-word suggestion like an apple and let them go. Usually after the first scene is over, the improvisers comment about how hard it is to do. And it is hard to do, at first. As with everything, the more you practice it, the easier it is to deliver. Upon the completion of the scene, we talk our way through it to help the improvisers understand the impact of statements that begin with one of these three words. "I", "You", and "We" are easy ways to start relationship building statements.

"I", "You", and "We" are easy ways to start relationship building statements.

When you start a statement with "I", what is going to follow will be information about yourself. It could be any variety of information, it could be about things you like, things you don't like, how tall you are, even how much you weigh. You get the idea, we could go on and on but just simply starting with the word "I", forces your brain to put together a sentence that gives out information about you. The more information you supply about yourself, the more comfortable everyone is going to be in the interaction. Keep it pertinent though, nobody cares about the weird dolls you collect, though arguably more of a hoppy than watching sports.

When you start a statement with "you", this will force your brain to create a sentence with information about them. That may seem a little brash when you first think about it, but we're not telling them what's wrong with them, we are telling them information that we assume we both agree on. Take the example of the group project gone awry.

Let's pretend that Scott bailed on his response and provided little information. Maybe he said something like this:

"Yeah, we are way off the timeline at this point."

Scott, just Castled (chess term, look it up you uncultured boob). This is an excellent opportunity to start a statement with "you". Consider if you responded with the following statement:

"You are known around here as being organized and on time with everything."

Assuming that's true, that's something that Scott already knew, and what you were doing is putting an emphasis on it. And by putting an emphasis on his quality, a positive one, you're creating a vacuum essentially saying to Scott, "I know it's not you, so what caused the problem?". Because we do it in the way of a statement, it gives Scott less of an opening to retreat into his brain to calculate his response. In a situation like this it's likely that there have been bad actors and he may also try to decide what is a good political move to make with his coworkers. And though we know those things happen in the workplace, they are counter to the type of productivity that companies are looking for.

"You" statements can also build relationships. In sales, the conventional wisdom is that if someone walks in with a Pittsburgh Steelers jacket on, to ask if they are a fan of the Steelers. Instead of asking a question to build rapport, consider making a statement like this:

"You must be pretty confident in your team to wear that jacket so close to Cleveland."

Good luck finding a person who will wear a Steelers coat that, when given the opportunity, won't immediately start bashing on the Cleveland Browns.

"We" statements are about us. The individuals in the interaction. Don't confuse this with saying "we would like to have you over for dinner sometime". That's really an "I" statement because it is a statement about you and someone who's not in the interaction. The "we" statements I'm talking about are you and the others in the interaction. Sales people should use them all the time. They sound like this:

"We obviously both share the desire to deliver a top level product."

The more commonality we find, the more comfortable the interaction, and of course as I've said maybe ten times already, the more comfortable the more unfiltered.

I, You, and We, are also great at eliciting a visceral physical response. If you use them in contradiction to what you think to be true, often they can elicit such a response. Let's again go back to our example of Scott. In your mind, you think Scott may have been victimized by a few bad actors in the group, but you're not sure who and you're not sure in what way. What you are sure of is that, though the timeline was to be monitored by Scott, he could not do so. So perhaps to push him into speaking to that truth, you deliver the following statement:

"You must be the weak link here Scott."

It may read a little harsh, but even if Scott isn't willing to respond honestly, it's very likely that you'll see an honest physical response to such a statement.

Opinions

Opinions are very useful on an improv stage and can be very useful in a life or work setting, but need to be much more calculated. Frankly, people really don't care about most of your opinions. And you know this is true because, mostly, you don't really care about other people's opinions, right? If you can avoid opinions about things you know are controversial, and opinions about things that nobody really cares about, opinions can be a great tool for building statements. One advantage that opinions have is they almost always elicit a quick response. Unless the opinion is complex. Remember, the goal is to keep them from retreating in their heads. You can state opinions you think someone will agree with to verify, or you can use opinions to state something that you think they won't agree with. Either way, opinions almost always get responses.

One advantage that opinions have is they almost always elicit a quick response.

Emotion

Using emotion in your statements might be one of the most powerful tools you can have at your disposal. They are also a little complex.

When trying to convey something with emotion, the worst thing you can do is act. Don't watch someone deliver something emotional in a show or movie and try to replicate that. There's a good chance that if the actor you saw created the emotion

The key to acting out in emotion is trying to feel the emotion.

43

well, it came from a very honest place in that actor. The key to acting out in emotion is trying to feel the emotion. When you actually feel something, even if you could bring it up artificially, your expression of that emotion is authentic to who you are. Though most people aren't trained actors, it is my belief that we watch enough acting in our everyday lives, that most of us are pretty accurate critics. In my experience owning a theater, audiences could always quickly discern an inauthentic reaction from a real one. It's uncanny. If you deliver something in a way that's inauthentic, everyone will know.

If you can deliver something with real authentic emotion, even if ever so little, it does a very interesting thing to the people in the interaction. People mirror emotion. They do this because emotion is a critical function of our unconscious retention of experiences. Think back to the snake. I'm betting most people reading this have never had a life-threatening interaction with a snake. You have however heard horrifying tales of snakebites. Perhaps you have known someone who has been bitten by a snake, or maybe you're just into watching nature shows and have learned of the perils of a snakebite. The stories of snakebites personal or otherwise and your consumption of snake nature shows get filed away by your unconscious mind. Depending on how they were

People mirror emotion.

presented, probably under an emotion. If our unconscious mind has a library full of the experiences we have had, the way your brain categorizes them is by emotion. The snake stories and shows get filed in the "Fear" section. Also in that fear emotion section are things that actually have happened to you. Perhaps you had an unpleasant experience with a dog or a cat. That would be filed in the fear section. I'm sure at some point you've been bitten or stung by some sort of insect. That goes in the fear section. These things go into the fear section and when you lift the rock and see the snake, your brain, in a fraction of a second, reviews the fear section and decides that the thing under the rock reflects that section best. That's how it creates the quick response in elevated heart rate.

Similarly, this is also how we empathize. When we notice an emotional experience with another person, our brain identifies their emotion without our conscious thought, and connects it to similar emotion that you have experienced. If you think that this is not how your brain works, think for a moment about a traumatic situation that you've been in. Maybe don't go too deep in the trauma, but something

When we notice an emotional experience with another person, our brain identifies their emotion without our conscious thought, and connects it to similar emotion that you have experienced.

moderately traumatic. Think about it for a second. Can't you feel some of those same feelings coming back? When you can add authentic and appropriate emotion to a statement, you trigger the unconscious mind of those in the interaction.

In the next chapter will dive into the elements of creating emotion and practicing it because most of it comes nonverbally. There are two verbal elements that are very important to emotions, and they are tone and pace. Tone has to do with the loudness and softness and inflection in your voice.

Try an exercise with me. This exercise is going to need to be done out loud and it will be a little silly, so if you need to find your way to a place where you can be alone, do so now. I'm going to give you a subject to talk about. I want you to imagine that you were addressing another person about the subject. When you do it, instead of using words, I only want you to use numbers counting up. Start at 1 and go to 50. I want you to express the following idea as honestly as you can:

Driving while intoxicated is a terrible thing that no one should do.

Elaborate on that as much as you'd like, but pretend right now that you are addressing somebody about this subject using only numbers.

Did you notice your tone? Did you catch

inflection in your voice? Try it again and this time try to pay attention to your voice as you wag your finger at the imaginary other person.

Pace is the rate at which you deliver information. I'd like to think of pace akin to orchestrating music. A great piece of music speeds up and slows down strategically it gets louder and softer. Music has been proven over and over by scientists to be an avenue to elicit emotion. Adding tone in pace to your delivery is one great way to deliver authentic emotion.

There are two verbal elements that are very important emotions, and they are tone and pace.

Use that exercise to practice both. Pick any subject you want to talk about and count from 1 on up while practicing tone and pace. In my theater we have people go from 1 to 100, try to expand to 100 after practicing a few times.

You Can't Spell "Pace" Without "Space"

Using silence strategically is worth its weight in gold. It's important to understand I'm not advocating for just sitting quietly. Rather, I'm suggesting that you understand the power of allowing silence as strategic moments in a conversation.

47

I've already mentioned the importance of stopping at the end of a statement instead of continuing on and softening what you said. Occasionally, there will be silence after you make a statement. This silence is the other person fighting against the vacuum and trying not to give in. This moment of silence is a negotiation between you and the other people in the interaction of consequence. The first person to speak, loses.

...silence is a negotiation between you and the other people in the interaction of consequence. The first person to speak, loses.

Though it would seem that this would invite them to retreat into their heads, it actually creates a different type of anxiety for them. It's the anxiety you feel when a radio station cuts out suddenly, when a show you were watching freezes unexpectedly. It's like a cliffhanger. It orients their brains toward the notion that somebody must be speaking at all times. This is something that improvisers struggle with early in their improv education, this feeling like there has to be talking constantly.

Unlike a radio station or a TV station, people cannot simply flip the switch and turn off the conversation to go to something else. I think you'll find

48

that the desire to fill the dead space is so strong that people will often start talking in an uncalculated way just to fill the space.

This negotiation is also an incredibly powerful way to quickly put the ball back in the other person's court. Let's pretend you're back in that party planning meeting. You've gotten to the point of putting a plan in action. Dale, who self appoints himself to be in charge of everything, says the following to Karen:

"Well, Karen. I guess we'll need to order all those cupcakes."

Let's imagine that instead of responding to Dale, Karen says nothing and looks at him pensively as if to say:

Yes, I suppose those do need to be ordered.

Do you think Dale has the self confidence to wait for you to finally say something? Nope, Dale says something. Maybe he goes on to ask you directly. Maybe he gets nervous and says:

"I'll see if Scott can do it."

Gotcha Scott.

Coulds and Shoulds

If you want to say something that makes people retreat into their heads, use the word "could" or the word "should" in a statement. Anytime those words get used, the person receiving that statement has to evaluate all the elements of it, because you just handed them some work. Consider the following statement:

If you want to say something that makes people retreat into their heads, use the word "could" or the word "should" in a statement.

"You should hang up lights for Christmas, most people in the neighborhood do."

That statement forces the other party to retract into their brain because there's a lot to consider. And they are going to be the ones, apparently, who were doing it. How many lights would we need? How long of a ladder would I need? How dangerous is this? How much is that going to cost? They wouldn't thumb through those things so hard if it weren't for you assigning it to them. Even if you use "we" to start the statement, they are at least sharing some work.

Coulds might be even worse. When you tell someone they "could" do something, it implies knowledge on your part that they apparently don't have. When you do this to a person where both of you know that you don't have special knowledge (like someone who doesn't own a business telling a business owner what they "could" do to get more customers.), it can be infuriating. Let's pretend that you get home from work and tell your partner or roommate this:

"Sorry I'm late for dinner, I got stuck at a train crossing."

To which they reply:

"You could take the other route instead. It goes under the train tracks."

Oh thank you, grand master of the atlas. That's how it feels to hear that, isn't it? It triggers emotion, likely connected to similar emotions created by that person, and makes you start thinking about how frustrated they make you. And there you are, deep in your head.

Feel free to try them out if you think I'm wrong, but "coulds" and "shoulds" have destroyed improv scenes for years.

Quick Summary

Start In The Middle

- When you initiate a conversation with someone, especially if it's purposeful, it's like your scene you're initiating.

A Baseline

- The more established your relationships with the people in the interaction, the more potentially comfortable the conversation can be.

I, You, We

- "I", "You", and "We" are easy ways to start relationship building statements.

Opinions

- One advantage that opinions have is they almost always elicit a quick response.

Emotion

- The key to acting out in emotion is trying to feel the emotion.

- People mirror emotion.

- When we notice an emotional experience with another person, our brain identifies their emotion without our conscious thought, and connects it to similar emotion that you have experienced.

- There are two verbal elements that are very important emotions, and they are tone and pace.

You Can't Spell "Pace" Without "Space"

- ...silence is a negotiation between you and the other people in the interaction of consequence. The first person to speak, loses.

Coulds and Shoulds

- If you want to say something that makes people retreat into their heads, use the word "could" or the word "should" in a statement.

5

Some Words Are Visual

Your Non-Verbals

It doesn't matter if it's improv, your personal life, or your work life, people get caught up mostly on what it is they say. Often ignored is nonverbal communication. Not only is it a major part of our everyday communication, it is also an incredible tool to couple with statements. Your ability to express nonverbally the emotion behind your statement gives you a powerful edge in communication.

In the prior chapter, I said that you need to create authentic emotion. It's easy enough to say that, but how do you do it? We had a great exercise for tackling this in my theater. The good news is it is something that you can repeat on your own with no one else.

In this exercise, we whittle down all emotion into four categories. Happy, sad, angry, and afraid. I've read arguments that there are more core emotions, but for this book, let's stick with these four. You'll be practicing each of those four emotions, but you're going to practice them on a scale. The scale is from 1 to 10, where 1 represents the lowest possible feeling of that emotion and 10 represents the most heightened feeling of that emotion. When we do this exercise in the theater, I spread all the improvisers out across the room and ask them not to interact with anyone else. I ask them to meander around the room and when I yell an emotion and a number; they try their best to connect to the feeling of that emotion as they walk around. So if I yell "Sad, 6" I am telling them to feel a moderate amount of sadness. If this scale seems odd to you, we actually do this in life, except we don't call it "Sad, 6", we call it dejected or something similar. Take a moment to walk around your room and feel "Sad,6". The exercise in the future is as simple as assigning yourself a different emotion and number, after you feel you have adequately settled into the previous one. This exercise not only helps you learn how to connect with, and display, varying levels of emotion, but it also helps you identify what levels of emotion might be too much or too little.

I advise in the beginning of most interactions of consequence; you start at a happy level four. I say this because it has been my experience that it is much easier to move from moderate happiness to any of the other emotions. In contrast, starting with one of the other emotions, like anger, makes it much more difficult for you to bring yourself to happiness. And since we're talking about communication strategically, it's in your best interest to start from the most strategic point. Think about a baseball player in a batter's box, they are trying to start at the most advantageous position for them to hit the ball. It should be no different for you.

My son and I were recently watching a new show. He's five years old and much of what he likes to watch are good guy/bad guy shows. We were watching such a show together and a new character entered that hadn't entered the show before. My son looked at it, turned to me, and said:

"Daddy he's a bad guy."

I asked him why he thought that was a bad guy and he said, without hesitation:

"Because he has a bad guy face."

Even my five-year-old son can identify a bad guy face from a good guy face. Don't be a bad guy. Even if you think it's cool to maintain some sort of stoic exterior, it isn't very strategic to start as the bad guy.

Their Non-Verbals

Most everything I have read teaching how to read the nonverbals, focus on knowing what means what. If their eyes go this way it means this, if they shift their shoulders in this way it means this. I don't think those are very helpful. In my experience, I never have to teach that at all, though I teach reading nonverbal as a major component of improv. The reason I don't have to teach it is exactly what I mentioned in a prior chapter. At this point in our society, people are avid watchers of things. We almost all have a device right in our pocket at this moment on which we could watch pretty much anything we want. And because the world of acting has become increasingly professional, the expression of nonverbals is something that you are very accustomed to watching. Unfortunately, you're not very practiced in watching and performing at the same time. That's where things get a bit tricky because the active performance, even if your performance is only being a part of a meeting, creates the feeling of being put on the spot. It's similar in a lot of ways to being on a stage, under the lights, in front of an audience. That creates a lot of anxiety, and anxiety is a hijacker of your attention. If your attention is bouncing between your anxiety and the fear it's producing, and your outward communication, there's not much space to pay

The more confident you are in a conversation...the more attention you have to give to something else.

attention to anything else. The more confident you are in a conversation and the more control you feel you have over your ability to contribute (hopefully this book helps you do this), the more attention you have to give to something else. Being able to do this is a significant advantage that the large majority of people cannot do. Even if they think they do. But if you can work on the scale, and get yourself to where you are comfortable enough to pay attention to the nonverbal signals of others, they will almost always tell you everything you need to know. People think that they are being guarded, but in reality they are constantly spewing unfiltered information. If you're looking for it, you'll find it. Sigmund Freud once said:

"If his lips are silent, he chatters with his fingertips; betrayal oozes out of him at every pore."

People are not good at hiding their emotions. The only reason they never get caught is because everybody else is so worried about their own anxiety and what they want to say, they're not paying any attention.

If you work at being in control of your nonverbal communication, and can turn your attention to the nonverbal communication of others, you will quickly become an excellent communicator. Be leery of deceiving yourself though. When I ask people if they think they are good at these things, most people say they are. It's not until I get them in a series of exercises that it's revealed to them that they're actually quite poor at it. So go into this assuming that it's going to require a lot of practice.

Dealing With Fragile Egos

I wish we could pretend that everyone treats one another with respect and sees each other as equally valuable. This is not always the case. In fact, it may happen the minority of the time.

It's also important to point out that some people are less well received when presenting themselves as competent. Though this isn't a book about bias, there are plenty out there and I don't feel I have to make much of an argument to substantiate my feelings on this.

If you've ever been in the position of dealing with a fragile ego, you know it's complex. Sometimes you need to offer an idea framed up as a question. You do this because presenting your idea as fact would be offensive to the fragile ego. If you phrase it as a question, they can claim the credit in their answer. I'm genuinely sorry for anyone having to deal

Giving someone a feeling of status is better than giving them the right to walk all over you.

with such a person, but I have a suggestion of how to change the statements you feel you can deliver in these situations.

Status is a subject I teach about in my advanced training. We exchange status all throughout the day without realizing it. Our collective brains feel the need to fall into a status hierarchy. Even when walking down the sidewalk, we make quick status exchanges and determine who will continue on their path and who will give way. Business meetings are packed with status exchanges. Though we don't consciously think about gaining status in a meeting, our animal selves typically launch into it for us. Leaning back in chairs, putting others down, these are examples of ways people unconsciously try to gain status in interactions. If you're dealing with a fragile ego, they're looking for others to recognize their status.

Giving someone a feeling of status is better than giving them the right to walk all over you. It appeases their ego and gives you the opportunity to present yourself how you'd like to. There are a few simple ways to give someone status.

Close Off Your Body

Our brains are triggered by displays of dominance. The bigger and more spread out someone is, the more our brain sees them as being dominant. When you close off your body posture, it makes it easy for the other person to puff out their chest a little.

Imagine a box sliding over your head, covering your body. The smaller the box, the better you're doing at this. When I need to employ this and am sitting across from the ego, I bring my knees together, lean forward slightly, place my hands folded in my lap, and allow my shoulders to roll forward. This routinely triggers an opposite reaction. It's almost like giving them the proverbial armrest.

I understand that this may read to some of you, especially those who have to deal with this frequently, as rolling over to a destructive behavior. You are, somewhat. But unless you want to pick a fight through HR, this is a way to give some feelings of status to the person desperately fighting for it. Your reward is in the long game.

Watch Your Tone and Pace

This is sneaky sneaky, but they deserve it. The trick here is to deliver a statement with all the tone, pace and non-verbal markings of a question. It may sound tricky, but after you practice this a few times, you'll get the hang of it.

Imagine a fragile ego you have to deal with. After you let the chill go down your spine, practice delivering the following question to them:

"Do you think it would be a good idea to get the group's feedback before deciding?"

Practice that question like you're wincing for a slap across the face. Practice it over and over until you have the tone, pac- and non verbal delivery down. Now, using the same tone, pac- and non verbal delivery, say the following statement:

...deliver a statement with all the tone, pace and non-verbal markings of a question.

"It's usually a good idea to get the group's feedback before deciding."

Practice that over and over until you can match the tone, pac- and non verbal delivery from the question to this statement. Do you feel like it would be harder for the other party to find this to be "too abrasive" or "bossy" or "speaking out of turn"? Combine this with the status tips and I think you'll find the ability to make statements in places that you previously would not have.

Quick Summary

Your Non-Verbals

- ...start at a happy level four.

Their Non-Verbals

- The more confident you are in a conversation...the more attention you have to give to something else.

- ...the nonverbal signals of others, they will almost always tell you everything you need to know.

Dealing With Fragile Egos

- Giving someone a feeling of status is better than giving them the right to walk all over you.

- ...deliver a statement with all the tone, pace and non-verbal markings of a question.

6

Almost Done

Parting Words

So much of communication is behavioral. I have over the years attempted to sit down and write books regarding all the behavioral aspects of communication that I've learned to teach. It has proven terribly difficult because we cannot learn many of the behaviors in communication through a book, but through experiential exercises. So, though listening, quick thinking, etc., are incredibly important, I have completely ignored them in this book. Those skills are foundational to the ability to communicate. If you want to be a better communicator, you need to look at it as if you are an athlete. Getting stronger in one area doesn't make you more athletic, all areas have to be exercised. Similarly, though there are mechanics to communication like the ones I have detailed in this book, mechanical understanding of something isn't enough on its own. A baseball pitcher needs to understand the mechanical aspects of pitching. But if that pitcher is not also athletic, it's unlikely they'll ever achieve any major success. Similarly, a person of great athleticism could never take the mound for a major league team unless they understood the mechanics.

If you're looking to advance your career or even strengthen your relationships, communication should be a major point of emphasis for you. At some point, you reach a terminal velocity in your skills. If you are an engineer, you will at some point become a brilliant engineer. But at that point, you may look around the room and realize that everyone is a brilliant engineer. When everyone has a high skill set, what separates a leader from a brilliant engineer is their ability to communicate amongst the engineers. Many people just communicate the way they always have and expect that at some point it would serve them in their success. After so many years of teaching improvisation and then teaching in corporate settings, I have found that few people work consciously to improve their communication skills. That said, for those who I have taught and have practiced the skills on their own, I always receive feedback about how much of a difference it made in their work and personal lives. It's silly to me we don't teach interpersonal communication as a part of childhood education. Some countries do, the United States does not. And yet, it seems to be a major obstacle in relationships of all kinds. So if you've gotten this far, don't stop now.

Remember, understanding is not the same as knowing.

Appendix

Summary of Summaries

Chapter 1
Let's Get Things Straight

Interactions Of Consequence

- An interaction of consequence is any interpersonal interaction one has with another person that could result in a positive or negative outcome.

Communication Is Not A Volume Game

- Communication is a precise art form. It's about delivering exactly what your audience needs to hear, exactly how they can best receive it, exactly when it needs to be delivered.

Understanding and Knowing

- ...people frequently blur the difference between understanding and knowing.

- Out of all the things you do in your life, communication is one that you do almost constantly from the time you wake until you go to bed.

Chapter 2
Question Everything

Nature Of Questions

- When you ask someone a question, you are asking them to retreat into their head.

- The more trusting an individual is in an interaction, the more willing they are to lose the filter and answer honestly and authentically.

Strategic Questions

- Do I want the other person to get in their head, filtering their response?

Questions Are A Cop Out

- ...your brain wants to be comfortable.

Chapter 3
Make A Statement

Statements Leave A Vacuum

- If questions cause people to retreat into their head to process and analyze, a statement does the exact opposite.

- Shut up. It heightens the gravity of the vacuum.

- When in the vacuum, people wind up saying giving up all sorts of unfiltered information.

Chapter 4
Statement Starter Kit

Start In The Middle

- When you initiate a conversation with someone, especially if it's purposeful, it's like your scene you're initiating.

A Baseline

- The more established your relationships with the people in the interaction, the more potentially comfortable the conversation can be.

I, You, We

- "I", "You", and "We" are easy ways to start relationship building statements.

Opinions

- One advantage that opinions have is they almost always elicit a quick response.

Emotion

- The key to acting out in emotion is trying to feel the emotion.

- People mirror emotion.

- When we notice an emotional experience with another person, our brain identifies their emotion without our conscious thought, and connects it to similar emotion that you have experienced.

- There are two verbal elements that are very important emotions, and they are tone and pace.

You Can't Spell "Pace" Without "Space"

- ...silence is a negotiation between you and the other people in the interaction of consequence. The first person to speak, loses.

Coulds and Shoulds

- If you want to say something that makes people retreat into their heads, use the word "could" or the word "should" in a statement.

70

Chapter 5
Some Words Are Visual

Your Non-Verbals

- ...start at a happy level four.

Their Non-Verbals

- The more confident you are in a conversation...the more attention you have to give to something else.

- ...the nonverbal signals of others, they will almost always tell you everything you need to know.

Dealing With Fragile Egos

- Giving someone a feeling of status is better than giving them the right to walk all over you.

- ...deliver a statement with all the tone, pace and non-verbal markings of a question.

About The Author

Justin Howard is an improviser, communication consultant, and now author. He has trained thousands of people in communication through improvisation methods. Justin dedicates himself to the transformation of others through experience based exercises and has little patience for arrogant blowhards in the business world. If you look around the internet, you may even find him in a variety of commercials.

To reach Justin about his training, visit www.emergeimprov.com.

The following pages are meant to be read as a flip book.

I

hope

you

enjoyed

this

book.

These

pages

are

added

to

make

the

spine

wide

enough

to

print

words

on.